Fernweh

Fernweh

A Collection of Short Uplifting Poems

Shrawni Akhauri

White Falcon Publishing

Fernweh - A Collection of Short Uplifting Poems
Shrawni Akhauri

Published by White Falcon Publishing
Chandigarh, India

All rights reserved
First Edition, 2024
© Shrawni Akhauri, 2024
Cover design by White Falcon Publishing, 2024
Cover image source freepik.com

The contents of this book have been certified and timestamped on the Gnosis blockchain as a permanent proof of existence. Scan the QR code or visit the URL given on the back cover to verify the blockchain certification for this book.

The views expressed in this work are solely those of the author and do not reflect the views of the publisher, and the publisher hereby disclaims any responsibility for them.

Requests for permission should be addressed to the publisher.

ISBN - 978-81-19510-63-4

"*To my mother, for her unwavering love and support,*

To my father, for instilling the values that shaped me and encouraging me to always pursue my aspirations,

And to my brother, for being my rock and support system during trying times, and for inspiring me to believe in myself even when the odds are against me."

Contents

Quiet Cold Night

When you find yourself blue,
hopeless and without a clue,
when you've lost all will to fight,
that's when your life seems like a quiet cold night.
When all dreams die,
and your soul begins to cry,
you can't feel the light,
and victory is out of sight.
That's when your life seems like a quiet cold night.
When you feel your lips quivering with agony,
and you start to question your sanity,
overpowered and overthrown,
when you've lost everything you own,
in the midst of a nightmare,
you're in a state of fright,
that's when you find yourself in the middle of a quiet
cold night.
When your heart keeps aching,
and your faith keeps shaking,
that's when you know,

it's time to let go.
When all you need is a hand to hold,
to feel the warmth,
and resist the cold,
when it's difficult to decide which path is right,
that's when you find yourself in the middle of a quiet
cold night.
But despite the darkness and the fright,
struggling against the current,
if you still have the will to fight,
against all odds,
like a flickering light,
you might just survive the quiet cold night.

The Storm Within

The peaceful facade,
the flawless skin,
the cheery bright smile,
and laughter akin,
are they enough to suppress the storm within?
Careful whispers and gentle gazes,
wrapped in the joy that delights yet hazes,
accentuating a subtle grace yet somehow muffling a
raging sin,
are they enough to suppress the storm within?
Promises of a joyous tomorrow,
hopes of that comforting warmth,
beaming laughter engulfing the sky,
yet a strange shadow somehow creeping in,
are they enough to suppress the storm within?
The pale moonlight shimmering in the night sky,
assuring you that a peaceful day is nigh,
but still the nightmares seeping in slowly stirring the
storm within.
Clutching onto the false mirage,

ignoring the piercing reality,
carefully painting the same facade,
not paying heed to the alarm bells,
you let your delusions win,
only to be left with the question:
are they enough to suppress the storm within?

Newfound Emotion

What is this newfound emotion?
Strange warmth seeping into the pit of my stomach,
downturned eyes evoking an odd motion,
flaring red cheeks not paying heed to any caution.
What is this newfound emotion?
Foolish heart beating loudly in my chest,
daringly ignoring the warnings in the back of my head,
slowly and steadily hazing out every heartbreak,
hushing out the piercing question:
"What if all of this is fake?"
But pushing aside all the warnings by my mind,
my eyes fixate on that smile so humble and kind.
Watching that face with much devotion,
I ask myself:
"What is this newfound emotion?"
As I gawk fondly at the crinkles by his eyes,
my brain decides to step in and remind me of all the
lies,
of all the treachery and deceit,
spelling out every word for me to heed,

reminding me of the mistakes I mustn't repeat.
But yanking myself out of this established notion,
I yearn to focus on this newfound emotion.
Careful eyes fail to look any other way,
staring boldly at a face as bright as the day.
And even when no words come out,
these are the thoughts my quivering lips were aching to
say:
"In the pouring rain and the shimmering starlight, your
eyes were the brightest,
and in the roaring thunder and rumbling lightning your
smile was the loudest."
But amidst this blur and all the confusion,
sinking into these thoughts as deep as the ocean,
I stood there wondering,
what is this newfound emotion?

Isolation

Why are we in this strange isolation?
Dark and cruel, evoking our every emotion,
so used to speed and confusion,
why are we amidst this estranged illusion?
Don't they know that we have no time?
To rest is forbidden and every second is worth a dime.
Blue skies and clean air are ever so brutal,
don't they know it makes us feel human?
We love our wrinkles and we love our frowns,
why do they want us to face the hurt we were trying to
drown?
We are accustomed to rage and power,
marking our presence and making others cower.
We are used to wearing our thorny crowns,
so why do they want us to care?
Why do they want us to slow down?
It's easier to live in a blur,
than to self-introspect and face our fears.
It's easier to hustle and join the daily grind,
than to show empathy and be kind.

When will they understand that we don't want to live?
That we just need to find a place and fit?
When we gaze at the sky,
we don't see a rainbow,
for our vision is hazed by everlasting sorrow.
Why don't they see that they are making us think,
that we are sailing on a boat that is bound to sink?
All our lives we were a part of this fight,
that kept us going, pushing us to strive,
but this isolation is making us believe,
that all of this is vague and there is more to life.
Don't they know that we have no zeal,
to pursue what we want and learn how to feel?
Can't they see our evident hesitation?
Could someone rise to the occasion and answer the
question:
why are we stuck in this strange isolation?

Wildfire

Where has it gone?
The audacious flame, the thunder, the spark, the
unstoppable desire.
Oh, sweet child, walking through these thorny gardens,
don't you miss that wildfire?
You have seen those grief-laden alleys and dreadful
ditches,
you have breathed in the air that makes mighty
mountains cower,
the one that gave you wings to fly above all the
confining hedges and restraining towers,
don't you miss that wildfire?
Where has it gone?
The zeal that made you destroy the hounds of darkness,
the whisper of courage that made you roar like a lion.
And the instinct that shielded you from all the
treacherous liars.
Wasn't that your luminous wildfire?
Come hail, come rain, or the screeching thunderstorms,

standing tall, oh child, you faced them all with might
that even warriors would admire,
never doubting yourself once, you marched on, relying
solely on that wildfire.
These noises that you hear, urging you to heed.
To heed to the futile norms, to heed to the bleat of
every sheep,
cautiously thrusting you inside a box.
Mark my words, oh sweet child,
even though they may seem urgent and dire,
do not let them put out that wildfire.
As with every drop of tear and blood,
you had carefully birthed this unflinching flame,
that glistens and glows over your empire,
as every once in a while, you look back at that graveyard
of trembling fears,
don't forget, how all of that transpired.
For you, my brave child, were meant to possess that
wildfire.

Hope is a Powerful Thing

Your heart is heavy with misery and despair,
shrouded with anxiety,
it yearns for care.
You are naked, vulnerable,
cowering and meek,
wounded and hurt,
every inch of you bleeds.
I know you live in the shadows to hide,
to save yourself from the ghosts,
you do not want to fight.
But if I tell you that somewhere around you,
there is still a starry sky,
will you gather all your courage and look for the beacon
of light?
I know your house is broken, and you have lost your
wings,
but somewhere in that building still, a little girl sings.
Humming quietly, the melody of clear blue skies,
if you blur out the darkness
ever so often, your mind can still hear that ring.

Reminding you what you already know:
'Hope is a powerful thing'.
I know that the demons are strong,
vicious and dark,
but wriggling out of their grasp,
you are still holding on.
I know that the lead sky is daunting,
but despite its darkness, you are still fighting.
I can see the horrors you face;
beneath the stormy clouds,
I see you struggling to pace.
But those sinful figures glaring at you,
they are only strong in this sinister haze.
So don't be fooled by the mirages they bring,
hope is a powerful thing.
You have lived in the land of agony for far too long,
with rivers of painful memories and oceans of despair,
all too familiar with them, you still stand strong.
Your weak form is relentless,
every now and then,
as the waves hit the shore,
it leaves you defenceless.
But even if it is tough,

I want you to look at the sky.
Even when you are numb,
I want you to cry.
As you stand at the bay,
let those tears of agony roll down as they chase your
monsters away.
Even when everything is gloomy and grey,
believe that those clouds will part someday,
the darkness will fade, and you will see a brighter day.
I know that right now, all lights are dim,
but chin up my friend,
hope is a powerful thing.

Strong Children

There they are, underneath the smoky skies,
with their eyes gleaming with perseverance and might,
carefully hiding all the hurt that lies behind.
With a heart soft as cotton, tucked away inside that
lofty mountain,
there they are, those strong children.
Misty orbs carrying scars and stories untold,
quivering lips withholding every unsaid word.
Trembling hands clutching onto their soul,
using their courage as their only ammunition,
there they are, those strong children.
Lost in the crowd of hollow men,
they search for burning fire in the pouring rain.
With every ounce of passion left in their veins,
they beseech warmth in a graveyard of shame.
In a century of vanity, they look for animosity,
mighty but broken,
there they are, those strong children.
Reciting the tales of happiness and hope,
while swimming against the current,

struggling to reach the shore.
Covering all their wounds, both new and old,
submerged a hundred times, but still who have risen,
there they are, those strong children.
The ones who have their hearts corroded,
with the pain, the hurt and sorrow overloaded,
still who march on blindfolded,
unaffected by the world that is cruel and rotten,
there they are, those strong children.

Something Real

The butterflies, the roses, and the pretty words,
the sweet talk, the lies, and the unworldly shimmer.
I heard you met the person with the pearls and the
glitter.
While they ushered you to the garden full of treacherous
rainbows and gleam,
did they hold your hand and ask you if you had your
meal?
I know that it's hard to resist that charm,
those big smiles and sugary words could probably mean
no harm.
But child, have you ever wondered,
beyond that veil,
beyond that thunder,
lies nothing but a shallow heart.
The one that is exciting,
but the one that can also tear you apart.
What you need is not the gold and the diamonds,
what you need is not a pretty picture of words but
action.

What you need is to feel,
to be happy, and to heal.
What you need is not to look at shiny rocks on your
hands with an empty heart,
but to gaze at stars, with hope and warmth.
What you need is not conniving lips and engaging little
games,
but the honest stares and dances devoid of any shame.
Not the illusions or ordeals,
my darling child,
what you need is something real.

A Little Piece of Home

The gentle swish of the mahogany trees in the backyard,

a slight whiff of morning coffee,

the cacophony of noises coming from the bustling

streets, gentle yet hoarse.

What does it feel like to get a little piece of home?

Is it the blue skies or the vivacious stormy nights?

Is it auburn autumn leaves wafting through the midday

air or a pair of warm welcoming eyes?

When you're anxious and alone,

what does it feel like to get a little piece of home?

Is it merely a cheeky tune or an old dusty road?

Is it a familiar scent or just a forgotten abode?

When you find your orbs teary, when you feel meek and

overthrown,

do you still search for that little piece of home?

Is it the audacious chatter of your old schoolmates,

or a rejuvenating banter and a homely embrace?

Is it getting petted by cold wrinkly hands,

or roaring waves and the golden sand?

Whatever your ordeal, my perturbed, lonely friend,
don't let your keen soul roam,
despite the hardships and the monotone,
look for that little piece of home.

Be Who You Are

They say, be who you are,

embrace your identity, your wounds, and your scars.

Let your truth drown the echoes,

beseech your courage, tell your story,

think not of the hurdles, but of the glory.

But me, my eager friends, am rather sullen,

embedded in the debris of appearances, covertly hidden.

The flashlight of hope, the beacon of dreams,

brilliantly shining o'er the unreachable beams.

These are the things I so desperately seek,

despite the shadows that are making me meek.

I sigh, I shake, but never surrender,

I swim through the waves that are taking me under.

They say, be who you are,

embrace your identity, your wounds, and your scars.

But my spirit is shrouded with invisible marks,

the truth I seek is impossibly far,

so, ask me not to embrace my demons,

for they are vile and will leave you marred.

I am better off behind these musty doors,
but to let the light in,
I leave them ajar,
because I heard you say - Be who you are.

Affection Is Not Our Strong Suit

Affection is not our strong suit,

for we have sifted through darkness and been doused in

despair.

Affection is not our strong suit,

because we are angry and damaged beyond repair.

Affection is not our strong suit,

because we see through the brick wall.

Clearly through the treachery,

and the lies, big and small.

Affection is not our strong suit,

but we know how to love,

to embrace the imperfections, to read the writings on

the wall.

Affection is not our strong suit,

but we know how to love.

Happy Ending

Sometimes I wonder if anything is real,
love, friendship, trust?
Are those just fancy words for people to throw around,
here and there?
What about the souls who care?
What about the hearts that love too deeply?
Are they just bound to suffer?
I guess we will forever be stuck in this never-ending
vicious cycle,
where one cares too deeply and the other turns a blind eye.
For people are flawed and humanity is being forced to die.
I pray there is more to this than what appears,
for we all deserve a happy ending, or so I hear.

I Identify as a Storm

I identify as a storm,
gloomy and fierce.
Roaring in the darkness, making earth cower,
yet illuminating the dark skies with lightning,
and soothing the scorched earth with rain showers.
I identify as a storm,
gloomy and fierce.
Often misunderstood, the epitome of fear.
Shaking the ground with tremors of terror,
yet rattling out a peaceful tune,
only a few can hear.

One of Those Days

Maybe you need to have one of those days,
where you ignore the alarm bells ringing.
When you throw caution to the wind,
when you take a breath and notice the birds singing.
Maybe you need to have one of those days,
when you sit down and savour your coffee.
When you are not beating yourself up,
when you are not chasing some insignificant trophy.
Maybe you need to have one of those days,
when you stop and let yourself breathe.
When you deliberately give up on that redundant fight,
and tell yourself,
everything is going to be alright.

Lead Sky

Trembling feet, carefully planted firmly on the sinking ground,
lifeless eyes desperately looking for a glimmer of light.
In between shuddering breaths, you still whisper - Better days are nigh.
Still standing underneath the lead sky.

Each morn paints the window grey,
engulfs your zeal and leads your demons astray.
Your vision is blurred with the haze of doubt,
suffocated, broken, and wary, you struggle to shout.
Though weak, you are still willing to try,
though defeated, you still let out a war cry.
Gloomy and dark,
underneath the Lead Sky.

Fret not, my friend,
for the sky spans across vaster lands,
what you behold is just a speck in the sand.

A day will come when you will gather your might,
suppress the storms and reach out to fly,
and even if the thunder roars,
against all odds,
you will burst out of the Lead Sky.

Shall I Unpack?

Shall I unpack?
All the stormy clouds and dark thoughts that remain
covertly hidden in crevices unexplored.
Shall I unpack?
The misery, the trauma, and the stories untold.
Should I show you the polished and pretty,
the shiny shell encasing all grim and gritty?
Or is it the raw spirit that intrigues you,
the untamed thoughts and the unidealistic view?
Shall I unpack and show you what's inside,
or tuck it away and just enjoy the ride?

Eye of the Storm

Like the eye of the storm,
alarming yet calm.
Navigating these dark alleys,
searching for a place which is comforting and warm.
Away from the noise,
away from the harm.
Relentlessly looking for a destination,
full of tranquillity and charm.
A destination devoid of shame,
free from the worldly norms.
I keep looking, keep moving forward,
to search for a place,
which, like the eye of the storm, is alarming yet calm.

Her Aura

Her Aura,
the story it tells,
of resilience and chaos,
of pure light and terrifying darkness.
It weaves its way through stony paths and pointy hills,
it swims across fear-infested waters.
Scarred but not invisible,
fading but still real.
Her Aura,
the story it tells,
of resilience and chaos.

The Heart Longs for What it Has Not Seen

The heart longs for what it has not seen,
a familiar presence,
calming and serene.
A spirit that offers warmth and understanding,
often persuasive, but never demanding.
An aura so imminent,
this heart cannot ignore,
one that beckons a ship back to its shore.
The heart longs for what it has not seen,
a familiar presence,
calming and serene.

Love is Gentle,
and Love is Kind

Love is gentle, and love is kind,

in all the struggles and all your smiles,

love is gentle, and love is kind.

It sees not just the flesh but the soul and the mind.

It hears not just the giggles,

but also the wails and the cries.

It admires your fervent desires,

and your relentless grind.

When you're in tatters or in luminous light,

during the day, and in the night,

love is gentle, and love is kind.

It Will Rain

It will rain,
even if the fire seems overwhelming,
even if you're scorched and in pain,
it will rain.
Even if the ground you stand on moans in despair,
even if your spirit is engulfed with flames,
it will rain.
For the relief-ridden clouds eventually chase away the
heat that destroys and maims.
Just hold on,
on your parched soul,
it will rain.

Guiding Light

Why am I on this path that is dark and full of thorns?
Why does everything lead to agony and scorn?
Do I not deserve to see the light?
Do I not deserve to seek redemption from this house,
pitiful and forlorn?
For all my life, I have been fighting this battle, wounded
and alone.
Do I not deserve a respite from these scars that I have
forever worn?
You say that I carry a light that needs to be shown,
on this path full of sticks and stones.
You say that I bear the flag of hope,
in the dark waters, I need to navigate the shore,
to show others that there is a way,
even if the road is garnished with troubles and dismay.
To prove that the mountains, tall and daunting,
can be conquered if we keep on fighting.
Perhaps I am on this path, which is dark and full of stones,
to weave through the darkness,
and show others that they are not alone.

Outside Looking In

All my life, I have been outside looking in,
intrigued, yet bewildered.
Keen, yet tattered.
Slowly and stealthily, dipping my toes into taunting
waters.
Peering from the cautiously woven mask of normalcy,
not to be heard, not to be seen.
I wonder if they know,
I am outside looking in.

Like Rose Petals

Soft yet majestic,
never sombre, always tart.
Coursing through the wind gently,
yet always leaving your mark.
You were like the rose petals,
never sombre, always tart.
Your playful smile,
every snide remark,
would light up even the gloomiest day,
and turn every frown into a chuckle,
masterfully, like a work of art.
Your presence, warm and comforting,
yet never devoid of banter and laughs,
you were like the rose petals,
never sombre, always tart.

Dear Teenage Me

Dear Teenage Me,

I envy you,

because you could dream.

You had emotions that were real,

and you weren't afraid to scream.

I envy you,

because your smile wasn't fake,

and you didn't have to worry about what you give or

take.

You believed in yourself and didn't need any help.

I envy you,

because you lived your life and didn't hesitate.

You ate what you liked

without worrying about your weight.

You weren't afraid to dance in the hail.

I envy you because you believed in fairytales.

And when your eyes would shimmer with hope,

you would just go for it,

without fretting about its scope.

Back when you still cared about your bucket list,

that was the time when you were still an optimist.
I envy you
because you thought life was colourful,
seeing the beauty in everything,
is what was truly wonderful.
You didn't care about getting a fancy dress,
back when your hair was still a mess.
When the only thing that mattered was whether or not
you were happy, when you weren't ashamed to act sappy.
Those were the times,
when you were as innocent as a dove,
when you believed the most beautiful thing in the world
was love.
I envy you
because you knew how to smile in dismay
while here I am cowering and hiding from life,
which is full of loneliness and shades of grey.
Even in despair and sorrow with hope,
your eyes would gleam.
I envy you
because you could dream.

It Is the Craziness That I Crave

It is the craziness that I crave,
the raw, uninhibited spirit,
fearless dreams, clear and vivid.
The will to go far without hesitation or shame,
the power to remain zealous till I'm resting in my grave.
Unfazed by human emotions,
I want to march through this unknown haze,
for it is the craziness that I crave.
All my life, I've been so afraid,
to embrace my demons, and end this charade.
To see the world for what it could be,
an ocean of opportunities, an endless sea.
Not for the fears but for the hopes,
not for the deception but for the love.
All my life, I was afraid to be wild,
desperately looking for corners to cower and hide.
Always playing by the book,
always seeing but never daring to look,

telling myself every day that I should behave,
never actually realising that it is indeed the craziness
that I crave.
Listening to everyone but me,
I let my fears break free.
Paying heed to every norm,
I let the sinful ghosts conquer my broken form.
Amidst the pain and the hopeless blur,
thankfully, I heard the voice of a little girl.
Chasing away the vicious hounds,
she told me to stand my ground.
To fight my doubts and see through the blur,
not to trust statistics and have faith in her.
To focus on my blessings instead of the flaws,
and to love myself for the brave little girl I once was.
Driving away all the insecurities,
she inspired me to be brave,
and convinced me to pursue the craziness that I crave.